THE HIGHLANDS
OF PAPUA NEW GUINEA

Published 1983
Robert Brown and Associates (Aust) Pty Ltd.
P.O. Box 29, Bathurst, N.S.W. Australia.

National Library of Australia
Card Number and ISBN 0 909197 37 7

Designed by Maureen MacKenzie

Printed and bound in Singapore
by Toppan Printing Co., Ltd.

BRIAN MILLER
THE HIGHLANDS
OF PAPUA NEW GUINEA

ROBERT BROWN AND ASSOCIATES

TO THE MEMORY OF JOHN BUCHANAN

Without the generous hospitality of many friends, students and village people, this collection of photographs would not have been possible. Special thanks are due to my mother who encouraged me to roam, to Maureen for her design and to Angela for her patience as I constantly travelled away from home.

CONTENTS

THE HIGHLANDS OF PNG 15

THE HIGH LANDS 16

THE HIGHLANDERS 36

THE HIGHLANDS TODAY 50

RITUAL 90

HISTORICAL PERSPECTIVE 122

FURTHER READING 126

*Eastern Highlands ranges in late
afternoon (1)*

*Homeward bound in the Tari Basin,
Southern Highlands Province (2)*

*A traditional singsing near Laiagam,
Enga Province (3)*

Dancers in action near Laiagam (4)

It has been a privilege to live for many years in these valleys amongst people with such rich culture and strength of character.

I hope that today's Highland children will not forget their warrior heritage, the strength of their forefathers and the beauty and colour of their rituals, as they stride into the future.

Brian Miller

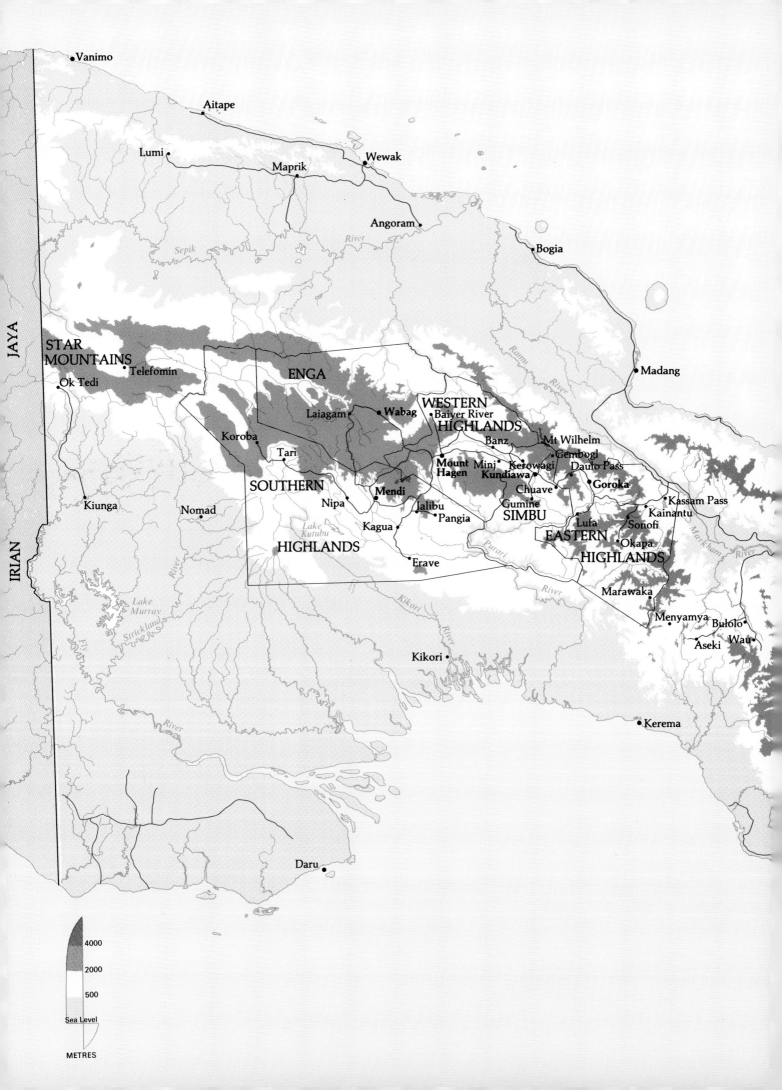

THE HIGHLANDS OF PAPUA NEW GUINEA

New Guinea, the second largest island in the world, has a massive mountain chain running along its centre. A vast, almost uninhabited lowlands rain forest flanks both sides of this mountain chain and, despite its location near the equator, the tops of the highest peaks are cold and icy. Within these mountains lie beautiful valleys, with an appeal all of their own, a climate like perpetual spring, and proud inhabitants.

Prospectors and missionaries began to venture into the fringes of the Highlands about 1920, but exploration was slow because the mountains were considered to be largely uninhabited. The Highlands of New Guinea made front page news all around the world in 1933, however, when the first plane, containing a party of gold prospectors, flew over these mountains. To their surprise they saw beneath them wide open valleys, a large population and widespread cultivation.

During the past 50 years these Highland people have undergone more rapid change than almost any people in the world have seen before, or perhaps will ever see again.

Although this book is devoted to the Papua New Guinea Highlands and its people, a similar landscape and life style extend across into the western half of the island, now the Indonesian province of Irian Jaya. It is a tragedy of colonial history that this beautiful island and its population have been divided in two.

Here is a place where two worlds exist side by side, where extremes of old and new come together, and where life is in a state of constant flux. Villages in the remote areas exist in perfect balance and harmony with nature, and hand to hand warfare continues in a nuclear age. Art is part of life, the body is the medium. Rituals are older than anyone can remember.

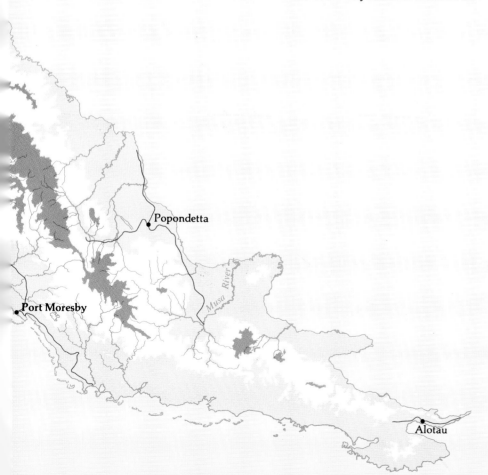

THE HIGH LANDS

Mount Wilhelm (4 509m), the highest point in Papua New Guinea, lies in the distance behind the rugged expanse of the Simbu Province. This view, taken from the slopes of Mount Michael, shows the settlement of Lufa below (5).

The countless rugged ridges, beautiful interlocking valleys and cool mountain air of the Highlands have had a powerful effect on the people. The lively character of the Highlanders is a product of these features which continue to provide a challenge today. How did this impressive landscape come about?

Continents of the world once formed a large single land mass which some 200 million years ago began to split up and slowly spread around the globe. The island of New Guinea was formed as a result of the Australian continent drifting steadily northwards and colliding with the Pacific Ocean floor.

Ocean floors are composed of much thinner but heavier rock than continents. As the Australian continent moved north, huge slabs of ocean floor were forced to slide slowly underneath. When one mass of rock overrides another, heat is generated from the resulting friction and regular earthquakes occur. As the rock slabs are pushed deeper, the heat increases, and the slabs begin to melt, providing the material for volcanoes.

The Highlands began to take shape about 180 million years ago when a chain of volcanoes erupted north of a newly developed submarine trough along the northern edge of Australia. Burdened with volcanic lava from the north and sediment from the continent to the south, this trough gradually deepened over millions of years. The Highlands began, not as a series of mountains, but as a huge sunken trough filled with sediment and lava.

Forty million years ago increasing pressure forced the trough filled with sediment to move upwards. New Guinea began to emerge from the sea. Volcanic activity diminished, while a new chain of volcanoes began to develop further to the north, forming the base of the New Guinea Islands.

Volcanic activity ceased throughout the region some 30 million years ago and most of the newly developed land sank back beneath the sea. New sediments were deposited on the sunken land and in the quiet waters thick deposits of limestone were built up from the bodies of marine organisms.

This quiet period came to an abrupt halt 14 million years ago when a volcanic chain burst forth again along the submerged Highlands. Liquid rock pushed beneath the sunken land and the Highlands emerged from the sea once more. The rock layers were thrust up to their present position in a series of movements which still continue. Although most of the Highland volcanoes have become extinct leaving peaks such as Mount Giluwe and Mount Hagen, there are still two areas of thermal activity near Tari and Menyamya. Regular earthquakes and tremors remind residents of the Highlands that all is not yet quiet.

Rapid uplift of the Highlands caused immense deformation of the rock layers which are everywhere faulted, folded and distorted. The accompanying volcanic activity brought from the depths below, vast wealth in the form of gold and copper. Today the uplift continues but high temperatures, high rainfall and steep slopes combine to wear the land down as fast as it rises. The decomposing rock and soil is swept down fast flowing rivers through deep gorges and laid out as silt on the flood plains below. The height of cliffs, the underground caverns, the landslides and slumps are as impressive as the uplift which caused them.

The tropical climate has reduced the exposed Highland rocks to layers of soil several metres thick. Tall dense forest covers the entire area, except for the tops of the highest peaks and the valley floors. On the cold mountain tops only grasses grow. People have cleared the valley floors, but most of the Highlands is so rugged that little impression has been made on it by man.

6

7

Early morning mist covers the Goroka Valley floor (8) and partly hides the township of Nipa (6). The morning cloud has broken over the massive Markham Valley showing the Highlands Highway beginning to wind its way up to Kassam Pass (9). Deep narrow gorges carry the waters of the Wahgi River out of the Highland valleys (7). The fast flowing rivers running off the Highlands, offer a vast potential for hydro-electric power.

8

9

Rugged ridges surround the upper slopes of Mount Michael (3 647m) which dominates the Goroka Valley (10).

Climbing Mount Wilhelm is a popular walk, starting from Gembogl (2 440 metres high) which can be reached by road from Kundiawa. The well defined track runs up the valley (11), past tiny lakes filling glaciated depressions. From Gembogl the return trip takes two days with a night spent in a hut beside one of the lakes.

11

The road into the Enga Province passes over the shoulder of the Mount Hagen volcano, giving views across the Highlands in every direction. Sharp peaks formed by glaciation decorate the top of the Mount Giluwe volcano in the distance (12). Another early morning view across the Enga Province (16).

The southern edge of the Highlands is characterised by high limestone escarpments, such as the Hindenburg wall in the Star Mountains (13).

The Wahgi Valley, Mount Hagen with typical late afternoon mist and rainbow (15). Evening cloud rolls off the edge of the Highlands near Bulolo (14).

Early morning Goroka Valley looking towards Daulo Pass (17).

18

19

Flattened ridge tops were usually the first sign of development, with feeder roads often linking the airstrip many years later. Mountains and gorges surround the airstrip of Kundiawa (18), the centre of the Simbu Province. The arrival of a plane is always an event for spectators — Wabag airstrip (19). Development work on the roads to Wabag (20), Laiagam (21) (23) and Gumine (22).

20

The road to Okapa snakes through the
Sonofi valley amid early morning mist
(24). Red grass in the Goroka valley
signifies the beginning of the dry season
(25). A narrow road from Mount Hagen
runs down the edge of a steep gorge (27)
and into the Baiyer valley, location of
an established bird sanctuary. Tea and
coffee plantations and cattle grazing
occupy much of the Wahgi valley floor
(28), the largest valley in the Highlands.

Multi-coloured tangket leaves (26) are
widely used by the Highlanders to mark
land boundaries, as a symbol for peace
and to adorn houses and themselves.

25

27

28

29

Flat land is so uncommon in the Highlands that most gardens are developed on slopes, often very steep (29). The staple sweet potato kau kau is grown in mounds, which hold composted nutrients and allow the heavy rains to run off quickly in the channels left between the mounds.

There are very few lakes in the Highlands. This one, Lake Iviva, lies beside the road to Laiagam (30).

Villages and hamlets normally lie along ridges with gardens on nearby slopes (31) (32). A variety of fast growing trees such as the Casuarina, are planted near the houses to provide shade and a continual source of firewood and fence posts.

A small village lying below the road to Gumine, Simbu Province (33).

After leaving the Goroka Valley, the Highlands Highway climbs over Daulo Pass (2 478m) before entering the rugged Simbu gorges. Small hamlets line the ridges on either side of this pass (34) (36) (39) (40). A spectacular range of vegetation, including the ever useful bamboo, surrounds most villages providing shade from the tropical sun (37) (38).

An early morning view across Mendi town (41) and across the Goroka Valley in the late afternoon (35).

The key to rapid development in the Highlands was the aeroplane, however it was the arduous patrols that established essential human contact and brought services to the people of the valleys. The patrols linked the Highlanders with the outside world and enabled them to move more freely across their own barriers. ›

A government patrol sometimes consisted of over 100 carriers with a few policemen and a medical orderly. The organisation was provided by Australian patrol officers (kiaps), but it was the Highland people themselves who cut the paths, carried the cargo and set up camp. Without the strength and guidance of these mountain people, exploratory work would not have been so rapid.

At daybreak a patrol sets off at a slow but regular pace. Cutting through dense bush, travelling across rugged gorges and crossing fast flowing streams makes for slow progress. Travelling through populated valleys and along existing tracks is considerably faster. The patrol usually stops mid afternoon and sets up camp before the rain sets in.

Today the large exploratory patrols have almost disappeared as the road network expands and helicopters provide access to difficult locations. However in the foreseeable future, there will always be a need for smaller patrols to provide contact, information and health services to the many remote settlements.

42

43

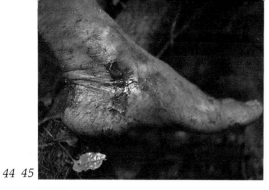 

 44 45

46

These scenes were taken on a large exploratory patrol in May 1978. This government patrol travelled from Okapa on the south eastern edge of the Highlands, down rugged unoccupied valleys to the Aure River (49) (50) which flows into the massive Purari River. Only one settlement of people was encountered during 8 days of walking (48) and many unexpected events occurred.

Leeches are an occupational hazard (44); the dense tall bush makes location particularly difficult (42) (47). Most cargo is slung along poles and metal patrol boxes help keep moisture out of valuables (46). Police in uniform add a 'bizarre' touch (43) and helicopters provide assistance in times of need (45).

47 48

9 50

THE HIGHLANDERS

In ancient times the New Guinea land mass was cut off from man and mammals in Asia by a sea barrier across the Indonesian chain. With the Ice Age came a lowering of the sea level and the exposure of land bridges. These factors, together with use of water craft, enabled people to move into New Guinea from the north and the west. The first inhabitants of the Highlands arrived perhaps as far back as 50,000 years ago, having retreated from the lowland coastal regions.

The original Highlanders were hunters and gatherers and the culture they developed was strongly moulded by the mountains around them. Travel was difficult and painfully slow in such rugged terrain. Some 6,000 years ago techniques of cultivation emerged. Clearing of forest on the valley floors began and pigs were introduced from the west. Well before the first European navigators sighted the coasts of New Guinea in the 16th century, the sweet potato had found its way into the Highlands from South America. This root crop eventually became the Highlander's staple food.

Geographical barriers and warfare between neighbouring clans have restricted groups of people to particular valley systems. And this produced a wide range of related but varied cultures and languages. The Highlanders are distinctive: small in stature with strong physique and intense clan loyalty. The active life style, plain diet and deep rituals have produced people with a special vitality. Children are given loving care and constant attention. And this close relationship between people continues throughout life.

For countless generations women have carried out the role of child-bearing, daily cultivation and pig tending. Men, the warriors, have specialised in such tasks as forest clearing, fence building, exchange ceremonies, and organising rituals.

People live in clan groupings, sometimes in villages but most often in hamlets or individual houses. Leadership status is attained by ambitious men who are superior in organisation, in the exchange of goods and in skilful speech making. Such *big men* may have several wives who increase his ability to produce children, crops and pigs. The strength of a clan depends on its leader who needs to work constantly at maintaining his status. The relationship between clans is a complex one of inter-marriage, exchange of goods and often warfare. A continuous pattern of agricultural cycles, rituals and exchange ceremonies is woven into daily life.

The people of Papua New Guinea regained their independence in 1975. The Highlanders, fortunately, can claim the shortest colonisation period in recent history. Today over one million people live in the Highlands with more than 60 indigenous languages between them. More than half the children now attend primary school. The language of instruction is English, but the link between most of the population is Pidgin English. There are still valleys virtually unaffected by the outside world except for a few steel tools and a radio. Some Highlanders live within the rapidly developing towns but the majority still live in villages and hamlets. Others have migrated to the lowlands, the islands and Port Moresby, the capital.

Life for the Highlander is a complex mixture of the old and the new and these rapid changes have not been without cost. A rapidly expanding road network is bringing development but also a high rate of accidents. Missions are bringing valuable health services and education together with new ideas that are eroding traditional beliefs. Cash crops are bringing money but this often results in the purchase of less nutritious foods and alcohol abuse.

To the outsider, these problems seem overwhelming but to the Highland people life is for living. Why concentrate on problems? Changes are accepted and new opportunities used to the full.

*The men of Tari are seldom seen
without some form of traditional or
modern adornment, particularly on the
head (52) (54) (55) (56) (57).*

*The young boy (53) is pictured at a
village exchange festival near Laiagam.*

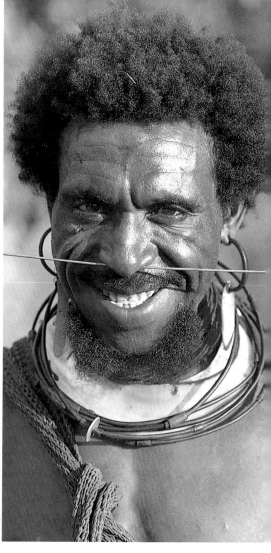

A group of men in a village at Nipa (58)
and a couple of men at a mumu in
Sonofi (59).

*Children on the roadside near Tari (60).
Relaxing after a hard day's work in a
mining camp, Star Mountains (61).*

63

A bright young girl from Sonofi, Eastern Highlands Province (62). A plastic bilum and a plastic hat adorn this character from Daulo Pass near Goroka (63).

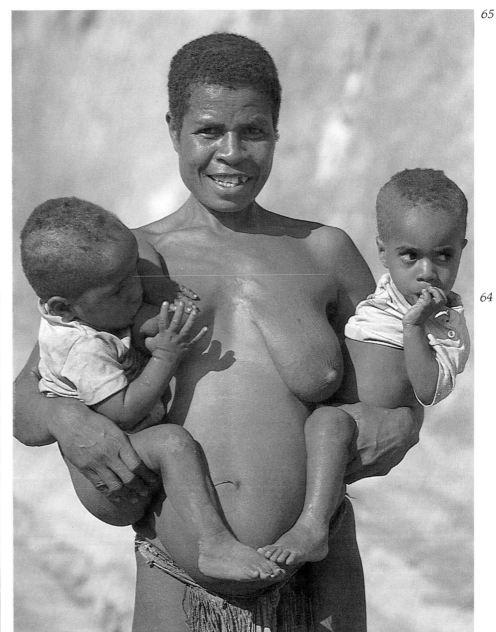

65

64

The Highlands women may not dress as brightly as the men, but they have character and charm of their own. The steep topography, continual walking and simple diet, produce a hardy, muscular population with a complete absence of obesity. The average Highland woman is a little shorter than 150 cm with men only a few centimetres higher.

A young girl from Sirunki, Enga Province who had been playing in clay (64). Mother and her twins walking towards Kundiawa, Simbu Province (65). A shy young girl from Tari (66). An Eastern Highlands woman at the Goroka Show (67).

68

69

70

71

72

An Eastern Highlands man (72) proclaimed Independence, September 16 1975, in his own particular way.

73

A colourful collection of men: from Mount Hagen (68), Chuave (69), Kerowagi (73) and the Star Mountains (70) (71).

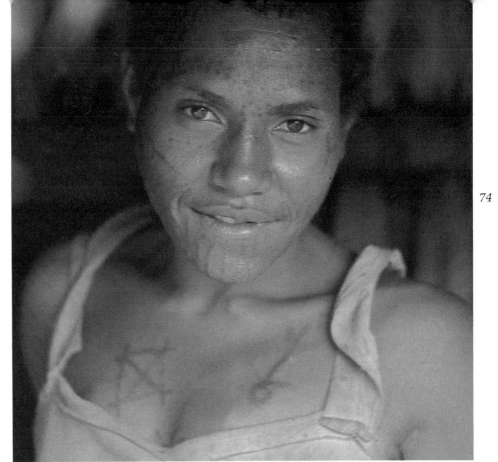

74

75

76

77

78

79

A woman from Gumine, Simbu Province (74). An old man and child walking towards Kundiawa (75). The boy and the gate (76) are part of the cassowary farm at Mendi. The 'smiling vegetation' is from the Star Mountains (77) and a young girl with traditional braids of the Bena Bena Valley, Eastern Highlands (78).

A majestic fully-dressed Southern Highlander (79) from Mendi.

THE HIGHLANDS TODAY

Tradestores, such as this one at Tari (80), provide an important link with the world outside.

In the mid 1950s the Highlands were finally linked by road with the coastal town of Lae. Today this Highlands Highway is sealed from Lae to Mount Hagen and extends westwards beyond Tari. Fleets of 50 tonne trucks travel up and down, bringing goods of every kind to the Highlands and returning to the coast with cash crops. Rough feeder roads spread from the Highway in every direction, each finally ending in a walking track which disappears over the mountains.

The pattern of life today is related to this expanding network of roads, although many isolated valleys are still served only by an airstrip. Small towns lie dotted along the Highway; smaller villages are found on the feeder roads and at the end of each road or beside each airstrip lies a tradestore.

For those whose valley is as yet untouched by road or plane, life continues in the traditional manner with little apparent change. But many young men have left the village to seek employment elsewhere. The closer the village lies to road or airstrip the more obvious the changes of the 20th century.

For the majority of Highland people subsistence agriculture still forms the basis of life. Garden plots are strongly fenced to keep out village pigs. New garden plots are cleared from the bush every few years. Sweet potato is the most important crop, providing the bulk of the daily food intake. Smaller amounts of sugar cane, pineapple, taro, maize, peanuts and leafy green vegetables are grown too. Small mammals and birds are caught from time to time and these, with fruit and nuts, supplement the diet. Pigs are eaten mainly on festive occasions.

Rural houses are still made of traditional materials although the customary round house is often replaced today with rectangular constructions. Cooking is done on a tiny fire in the centre of the hut. The smoke finding its way out through the thatched roof. The cooking fire embers never seem to die and give warmth in the cool mountain nights. Houses are usually built along ridge tops, making them easier to defend but requiring continual trips to the nearest stream for water and washing.

The Highland climate promotes plant growth throughout the year and life revolves around continual cultivation cycles. Most people produce a few cash crops which are trucked to the nearest centre and sold to purchase various consumer goods. For most Highlanders, the tradestore is the link with the outside world.

On market days the towns are flooded by thousands of villagers. Rows of shops are the main attraction, along with sporting facilities, social services and instant communication with the rest of Papua New Guinea. Almost without exception, each town has grown around a busy airstrip, providing regular daily links with the rest of the country. From dawn to dusk small planes link the distant centres.

Traditional transportation is by foot, with goods beng carried in string bags on the backs of the women. Animal transportation has never been part of their culture and a bicycle is of little use on a mountain track or a rocky road. The first wheel that most Highlanders would have seen was attached to a plane, and today the people step in and out of planes and trucks, without pausing to consider the technological leap that has transformed their lives.

Only a few years ago there were regular government patrols, which provided links with the villages and a control, imposed from the outside, on the pattern of life. Today, much of that has disappeared and has been quickly replaced by provincial politics. Many traditional leaders are now local politicians and a new system is being established. So many changes in so few years. This last change, however, is being handled by the Highlanders themselves. They are rapidly becoming experts in change itself.

Small aeroplanes have been the key to rapid development in the Highlands and almost 100 airstrips have been built since contact began. Air services, which underwent rapid expansion, now face increasing competition from the improving road network. Some airstrips have already closed. However, the plane will remain an essential component of daily life in the Highlands for many years to come.

Aeroplanes enabled the Highlands to develop as a whole, with inhabitants of each major valley building their own strip. Without the plane, development would not only have been much slower, but would have been restricted to the expansion of roads. Today Air Niugini serves the main centres, while Talair is the main operator of light aircraft (81) (82). The missions have their own air service network and helicopters are playing an increasing role in assisting development in inaccessible localities.

83

The township of Goroka (83) viewed from the upper slopes of Mount Otto (3 500m). Goroka lies in a large valley completely surrounded by mountains. This town, the second largest in the Highlands, has a wide range of amenities, services and educational institutions. Construction of the airstrip seen below was organised by the American forces in 1943 and built with hand labour by 1000 men in seven days.

85 86

87

88

89

Almost without exception, the Highland towns have developed around an airstrip, as illustrated at Mendi (84). Each town lies in a particular valley and is interconnected by the Highway. A mixture of tradestores, shops, small supermarkets, and services such as communications, health, markets and garages attract a continual flow of villagers.

Scenes from Mount Hagen (85) (88), Goroka (86) (89) and Tari (87).

The Highlands Highway near Chuave, Simbu Province (90).

(overleaf)

Markets provide a ready flow of cash for villagers, an abundant daily supply of fresh vegetables for the town dwellers and a meeting place for all. The mild climate of the Highlands allows continual production of almost any kind of vegetable. These scenes are from the markets at Goroka (91) (93) (94) (96) and Tari (92) (95) (97).

93

94

95

96

97

98

99

100

10

102

103

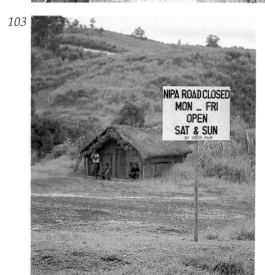

104

105

Improving the road network is an important aspect of development today. Volcanic rock is used for most roadbuilding, although there is widespread use of limestone in the Southern Highlands (98) (102) and Simbu (101).

Development continues on the road to Laiagam (100) and Nipa (103), while travellers head for Mount Hagen (99) and Goroka (105). A temporary blockage on the Highway near Kundiawa (104).

Card playing is a time consuming pastime throughout the Highlands. This group is playing on the roadside near Tari (110). A variety of team sports are popular with the Highlanders, particularly Rugby League (106). In Goroka, the Minogere pool (107) and racecourse (109) provide different forms of recreation. A raft and occupants floating in a stream behind Wabag (108).

106

107

108

109

Rapid development of schools continues in the Highlands and a wide variety of institutions have been established; ranging from the newly developed, such as Minj Day High School (112), to the Secondary Teachers Training College at Goroka (119).

17

16

Today approximately half of all primary age children go to school and about half of those go on to secondary school. All primary school teachers and most secondary teachers are Papua New Guineans. About half the schools are run by missions and half by the government, although all are under one Education Department.

118

119

Sonofi Primary School (113) and Chuave High School (111) are typical primary and secondary schools. Various school activities at Nipa High School (115) (116) (117), Tari High School (114), Kerowagi High School (118) and Mendi High School (120).

120

*Quiet meditation in the Catholic church
at Tari, Southern Highlands Province
(121). The cross (123) marks a burial site
overlooking the Catholic Notre Dame
High School, Baiyer River road,
Western Highlands Province. An
outdoor Lutheran service takes place on
Daulo Pass, overlooking the peaceful
Goroka Valley (122).*

*The old Lutheran church (124) (125) at
Daulo Pass has weathered the tropical
climate for many years. Sunday service
is an event for young and old alike.*

Missionary involvement has had a significant effect on development in the Highlands. Like most other contact situations, the missions have brought both problems and benefits.

A missionary walking around the streets of Goroka in his own unusual way (126). In a river below Laiagam, a remote locality in the Enga Province, a baptism took place with music blaring from loud speakers nearby (127).

Many missions have provided a lengthy and valuable contact with rural people and developed a network of health and education services. Father Niles has been working for the Catholic mission near Kundiawa since the 1930s, contributing greatly to the understanding of local custom and languages (128). The Lutheran hospital in the Enga Province is typical of many mission hospitals which serve the rural people (129). Rural mission stations, such as the one near Tari, are virtually self sufficient in daily food requirements (130).

126

127

128

129

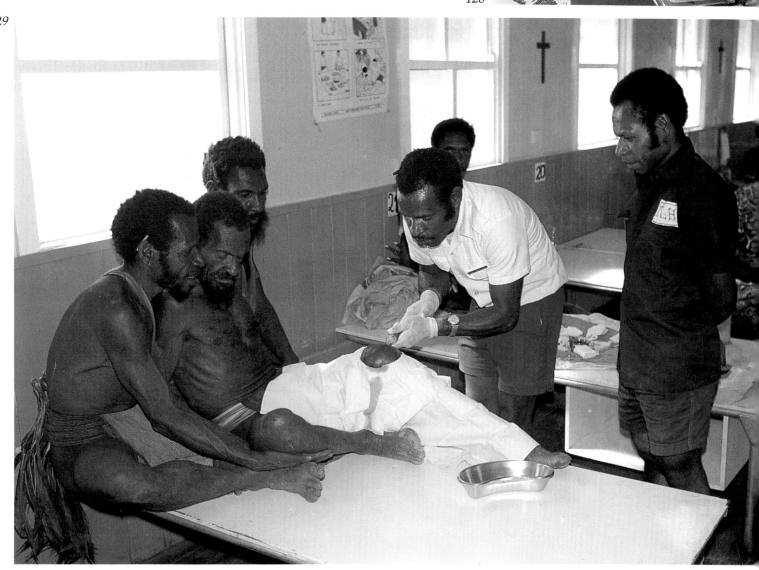

130

131

132

133

A woman near Goroka begins a long daily walk to the market (131), while youths stroll through a village near Banz (132). Early morning mist is dispersed as the sun rises over a village on the road to Okapa (133).

A typical Eastern Highlands village on a ridge near the top of Daulo Pass (136). High tension electricity cables, carrying power through the Simbu Province to Highland towns, have little benefit for those who live under their path (134).

134

In the Tari basin, gardens are divided by deep drainage trenches, which often have gateways opening on to the road (135).

135

140

141

A log bridge is the normal way of crossing small streams, such as the one at Sonofi, Eastern Highlands Province (137). There is no shortage of streams for washing in the Highlands and the strong sunlight provides drying while you wait (138).

Children arriving home at their house on the road to Okapa (139). When the days work is over, the fire is the centre of attraction (140). A little house in the bush on a narrow ridge below Gumine High School (141).

142

Highlanders' huts are warm at night and cool by day. A small fire in the centre is surrounded by a low sleeping platform. The timber frame is covered with flattened, woven pit-pit walls and a thick thatched kunai grass roof. Sonofi village Eastern Highlands Province (142) (143).

Vehicles are usually bought communally and this new arrival is having a garage constructed by Daulo Pass villagers (147). The elderly woman and man are residents of Sonofi village Eastern Highlands Province (144) (145).

Pigs normally roam free but are tethered when taken from place to place (146). Strong timber fences are built to keep pigs out of garden plots (149). Goats and their owner rest beside the Highlands Highway in the Simbu Province (148).

147

148

149

150

151

Subsistence gardening is practised throughout the Highlands, with garden plots being used for about 4 years before being left fallow. This plot of land at Sonofi is being cleared with the help of fire (151) (152) and in a few months time will look like the plot nearby (150). The technique of firemaking is certainly not lost, as shown by a Sonofi man (153) (154) (155) (156).

152

(overleaf)

A small ridge top plot near the top of Daulo Pass (157); and a girl with produce from Okapa (159).

Men help break open new ground but women do most of the cultivation. These women near Gumine are tilling a plot of sweet potato mounds (158). Near Gumine High School a woman brings home kunai grass for a roof (160).

153

154

155

156

158

159

160

161

162

163
164

165
166

167

168

169

The Highlands' bush with its tropical climate contains a colourful variety of flora and fauna (163) (164) (165) (166) (168). The tree kangaroo (167), goura pigeon (161), frogmouth (169) and cassowary (162) are well-known examples.

Layers of limestone, often thousands of metres thick, lie along the southern edge of the Highlands. The ground below is riddled with caverns and large rivers frequently disappear into sinkholes (170).

170

171

172

Coffee, first introduced to the Highlands in the early 1950s, is now a major agricultural export earner. The beans must be hand picked (172) (175) to ensure that only the fully ripened red berries are selected (171).

Once picked, the cherries are crushed to expose the beans which are then washed, dried in the sun (173) and sold to the factory for roasting. Half the coffee is grown in small village plots, while the rest is produced in plantations (174). These scenes are in the Goroka Valley, the centre of the Highlands coffee industry.

173

174

175

Mount Elimbari in the Simbu Province is a landmark well known by Highway travellers (176).

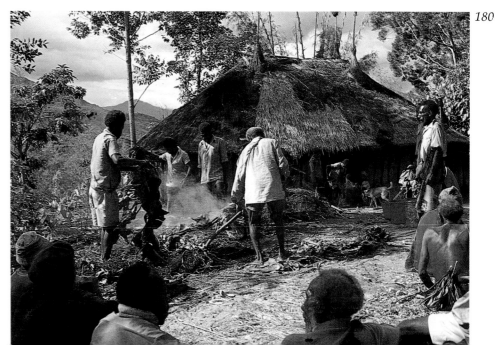

181

182

Pigs are eaten mainly on special occasions and cooked with vegetables in a shallow earth oven or mumu.

The mumu *begins with a large open fire heating stones and boulders, which are then rolled into a shallow pit. Layers of leaves, vegetables and meat cover the heated stones and a thick layer of soil on top forms an effective steam cooker, which is left for several hours with occasional additions of water. These* mumus *took place at Watabung (178) (181), Daulo Pass (180) (182), Goroka (183) and Wabag (177) (179).*

183

RITUAL

The rugged ridge tops of the Highlands are impressive but it is the spectacle of dance and dress that dazzles the outsider. Village life in the mountains is not easy. It is a continual struggle of manual work and ceaseless cultivation, but this is balanced by ritual, body decoration and festivities. These festivities are an integral part of the cycle of life.

Exchange — of pigs, shells and food — is vital to the Highlanders, and has important social consequences. Continual exchange has a mediating influence between opposing clans, enabling disputes to be settled and maintaining an overall balance of power. In times of hardship, those leaders and clans who have accumulated a surplus, help those in need. The form of exchange ceremonies varies from valley to valley, exchanges occur more often where the population is dense. Exchange festivals are often preceded by years of negotiation with consultations between clans becoming more frequent as the exchange date draws near. And the cycles of exchange continue as obligations are passed from generation to generation.

Marriage is usually between neighbouring clans and negotiations may take many months before agreement is reached upon the exchange of goods and the bride. There are many other occasions where festivities occur: cult ceremonies, fertility rites, initiations, settlement of disputes and now civic events such as the opening of new buildings. A feature of all these occasions is body decoration, including the elaborate and beautifully arranged forms of head-dress.

Body decoration is a group activity. It is a public show of strength and power. The more elaborate the dress the more impressive the effect as a clan marches into the *sing sing* ground. The form of dress varies from valley to valley, although there are distinctive regional patterns in the larger valley systems. A wide variety of material is used: feathers and plumes, fur, wigs, shells, bones, pig grease, ashes, oil, grass, leaves and earth paints. Today, except for the isolated valleys, it is also common to find trade store products such as paint, cloth, beads and even Christmas decorations!

Highlanders are masters of body decoration. Feathers and plumes are highly prized and handed down through generations. Sometimes they are exchanged, and they are always carefully stored between ceremonies. Decoration is largely a matter for the men, although girls or young women often take part, and in some areas older women participate. While full dress is reserved for the main exchange ceremonies and festivals, parts of the dress — perhaps a few feathers — are often worn during preliminary negotiations. Art in the form of carving or painting is seldom practiced by the Highlanders, although arrow heads are carved and beautiful weaving is found both in the string bags, *bilums*, and in the walls of houses.

Rituals relating to death require different forms of decoration. Instead of oil, mourners smear clay on their bodies to produce a dull, unattractive effect, far removed from the colourful adornment for dance. A death is followed by a series of rituals and gatherings enabling the family grief to be shared by the clan. The death is accepted in a series of well defined stages. Reverence for ancestors is an important part of most Highland cultures and the world of the spirits is a very real one.

Geologists can explain the rise of the mountains; anthropologists can study the way of life; but only the Highland people themselves possess the secrets of their rituals. Today their rituals face a serious challenge from the impact of modern life and imported beliefs. Few of the missions are sensitive enough to incorporate the ritual into modern worship. It seems that the Highland people are aware of and respect — far more than the average modern man — the power of nature and the unknown.

Dancers from Tari, Southern Highlands
Province.

Preparation for dance begins at dawn
with full decoration taking hours to
complete (186) (187) (188) (189) (191).
The dancers are smeared with tree oil
(185) before going out to perform (190).

The Huli people of the Tari basin are
known for the variety and beauty of
their wigs.

187   188   189

191

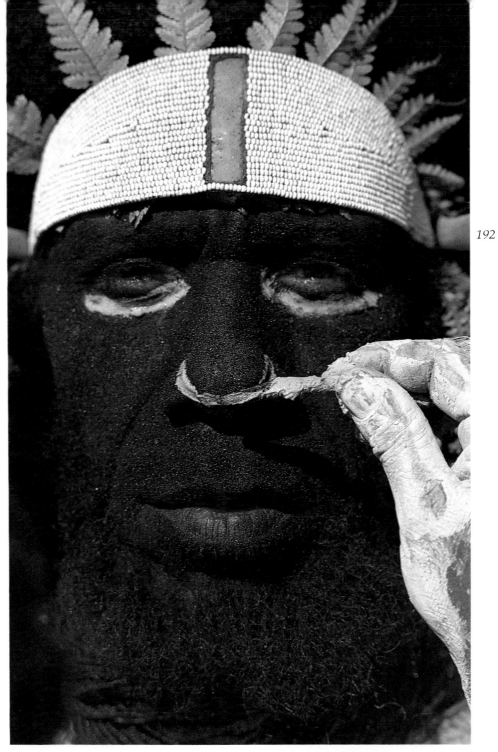

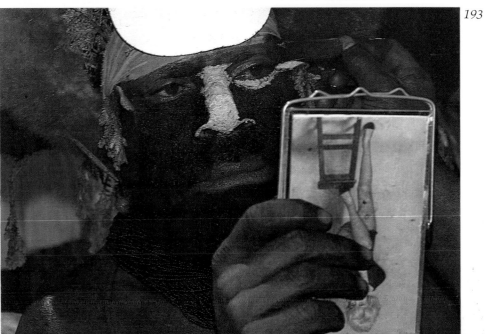

The road into the Enga Province climbs up the lower slopes of the massive Mount Hagen volcano, which lies in the distance. A small extinct volcanic cone lies in front of the Mount Hagen peaks (194).

Villagers from throughout the Enga Province gather for Lutheran church anniversary celebrations (192) (193) (195) (196).

194
195

196

Enga Province tribesmen provide a striking contrast with their surroundings. (197) (198).

Clay is smeared on the body, while the faces are covered with powdered charcoal mixed with water. The wigs are made from a framework of vines and are covered with clippings of hair from the dancer. Tall black plumes from one of the many varieties of Bird of Paradise, tower above the wig.

Leg bones from the large cassowary protrude from above the ear, while a single feather from the King of Saxony Bird of Paradise encircles the chin. Some of the dancers have a large pearl kina shell hanging on their chest and rows of tiny nassarius shells adorn the forehead.

Snake skin covers the heads of the drums or kundus and dabs of beeswax on the skin enable drums to be tuned.

There is no lack of innovation when it comes to dress (199).

A variety of dancers from throughout the Enga Province (200) (201) (202) (203) (204) (205).

203

Every even-numbered year, the Goroka
Show provides a major attraction for
villagers and tourists alike. Visitors in
the stand (206) have an uninterrupted
view of the arena.
(overleaf)

204

205

214

215

The show lasts two days and thousands of tribesmen from throughout the Highlands take part. Prizes are awarded for the most impressive traditional dress and the show now plays an important part in preserving the rich and varied cultures. These scenes (207) to (217) show something of the spectacle.

216
217

Dress, dance and colour at the Goroka
Show (218) (219) (220).

219

220

224

225

226

Tall bamboo frames covered in chicken feathers are worn by some villagers who live near Goroka (222). The grass beads (223) are normally worn by women in mourning. A set of red plumes (221) from the well known Raggiana Bird of Paradise. Simbu warriors with their richly coloured head-dresses provide a show of strength (226) (224).

The show provides plenty to catch the photographer's eye (225).

Masses of dancers at an exchange festival near Ialibu, Southern Highlands Province (227) (228). A Ialibu tribesman wears a large bailer shell on his chest and rows of tiny nassarius shells across his forehead (229).

230

Ialibu dancers with their distinctive heavily adorned aprons (230) (231).

Precision marching at a Ialibu exchange festival (232) (233). Women performing near Wabag (234).

Exchanges today involve not only pigs and produce but also large amounts of money. Here we see several thousand kina attached to bamboo poles being carried to a neighbouring village near Kundiawa (235).

Payment for a bride is publicly displayed, at a village on the Highlands Highway near Chuave (236) (237). Negotiations to arrange a marriage and confirm a bride price normally take several months.

237

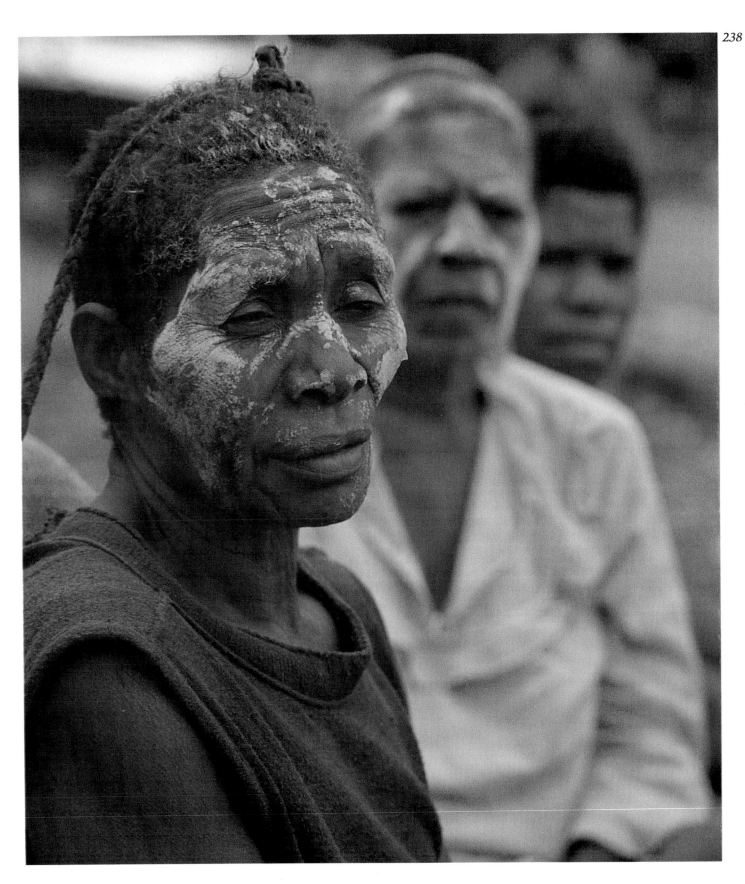

239

A funeral gathering at Kiamuga village Asaro, Goroka valley. The widow (238), whose husband was the 'big man', is supported by family and friends.

Women prepare food for the feast (239) while nearby a group of men sit and contemplate (240).

240

241

A group of villagers from Watabung travelled over the Daulo Pass to pay their respects at the Kiamuga village funeral (241) (242) (243).

A participant at the Goroka Show (244).

243

242

An exchange ceremony near Daulo Pass, Goroka.

HISTORICAL PERSPECTIVE

50,000 B.C.	The first settlement in the Highlands may have occurred about this time.
1545	Inigo Ortiz de Retes, a Portuguese, was the first European to sail along the north coast of the mainland he named New Guinea. During the next 200 years there were various visits to New Guinea by navigators and explorers from Spain, Portugal, France, Britain and Holland.
1793	British East India Company took formal possession of a portion of New Guinea.
1800s	The outline of New Guinea was now appearing on world maps.
1828	The western half of New Guinea formally annexed by the Dutch.
1873	Port Moresby located and named by Captain Moresby.
1884	South Eastern New Guinea proclaimed a British Protectorate.
1885	German New Guinea formally annexed by Germany.
1888	Annexation of British New Guinea proclaimed.
1906	British New Guinea became a Territory of Australia and was renamed Papua.
1914	German New Guinea occupied by Australian troops at the outbreak of World War I.

HIGHLANDS CONTACT BEGINS . . . . .

1919–20	Missionaries Lehner and Pilhofer, contacted villagers on the eastern fringe of the Highlands above the Markham Valley.
1921	Australia given a League of Nations mandate to administer German New Guinea.
1926–27	Missionary Leonhardt Flierl contacted villagers in the headwaters of the Purari.
1927	Champion and Karius explored the upper Fly and Strickland rivers, then travelled across the Highlands and down to the Sepik.
1928	A gold prospector, Ned Rowlands, established a camp in the Arona valley near Kainantu.
1929	Missionaries Bergmann and Pilhofer reached the Bena Valley near Goroka.
	The first aeroplane flight into the Highlands surveyed eastern fringe valleys.
1930	Gold prospectors Michael Leahy and Michael Dwyer entered the Eastern Highlands and followed tributaries of the Purari down to the Gulf of Papua.
	Prospector William McGregor entered the fringe of Enga Province from the Sepik.
1932	An airstrip was built in the Bena Bena valley.
1933	The Leahy brothers historic flight over the Simbu and Wahgi valleys 8 March.
	Michael Leahy, Dan Leahy, Jim Taylor and Ken Spinks left the Bena Bena valley 28 March on the first major patrol through the Highlands. They travelled through the Simbu and explored the area surrounding Mt Hagen for several months.
	Father Schaefer visited Kerowagi late in 1933 from the Catholic station at Bundi.

1934	Another party of Catholic priests led by Father Ross walked through the Simbu to Mount Hagen and then returned to set up a station at Mingende (near Kundiawa).
1935	Government Officers, Hides and O'Malley, entered the southern fringes of the Highlands on a patrol from the Gulf.
1936	The English Fox brothers travelled from Mount Hagen through Wabag to the head-waters of the Sepik near the Dutch border, and back through the S. Highlands.
1938–39	Jim Taylor and John Black led a patrol which explored the area between Mt Hagen and the Dutch border for 15 months, using air drops and wireless — claimed as the largest, longest and best equipped patrol ever mounted in New Guinea.
1939	A Government Office established at Goroka along with a small airstrip (where the Teachers College stands today).
1942	The Territory of New Guinea was invaded and occupied by the Japanese. The Highland valleys were not invaded but sporadic bombing occurred near Goroka.
1943–44	Mainland New Guinea recovered from the Japanese by American/Australian Forces.
1944	A jeep road opened between Kainantu and Goroka.
1946	Australia given authority by United Nations to control New Guinea.
1949	Papua and New Guinea were merged by the Australian Parliament to become the Trust Territory of Papua and New Guinea.
1951	The Legislative Council of Papua New Guinea was inaugurated.
Mid 1950's	Possible to travel by road from Lae to Mount Hagen.
1963	The Legislative Council replaced by a House of Assembly with 64 members to govern Papua New Guinea.
	Western New Guinea became a Province of Indonesia and was renamed West Irian — later Irian Jaya.
1966	Highlands Highway upgraded. Transport of cargo by road into the Highlands became more economical than by air.
1971	The combined Territories of Papua and New Guinea were officially named Papua New Guinea and a National Day, Flag and Emblem proclaimed.
1973	On December 1 Self Government was established.
1975	On September 16 Papua New Guinea became an independent sovereign state.
1977	First National Elections since Independence. Michael Somare appointed P.M.
	Interim Provincial Government adopted by Eastern Highlands, Simbu and Southern Highlands Provinces.
1978	Interim Provincial Government adopted by Enga and Western Highlands Provinces.
1980	Sir Julius Chan became Prime Minister.
1982	Michael Somare re-elected Prime Minister.

A small village near the Goroka Valley.

FURTHER READING

This selected list will assist those who wish to obtain more information on the Highlands or read about the culture and way of life.

ENCYCLOPAEDIAS

Encyclopaedia of Papua New Guinea (3 Volumes). Ed Peter Ryan. Melbourne University Press 1972.
Although now several years out of date, this is still the only encyclopaedia of Papua New Guinea and a very useful general reference.

ATLASES

Papua New Guinea Resource Atlas. Ed Ford. Jacaranda Press 1974.
A large format full colour atlas.

Papua New Guinea Atlas — A Nation in Transition. Ed D King and S Rank. Robert Brown and Associates, Australia 1982.
This atlas contains maps on a wide variety of topics including lists and locations of all intensive ethnographic studies undertaken since 1969.

Jacaranda Papua New Guinea School Atlas. Niugini Press 1980.
A simplified school atlas.

MAPS

The National Mapping Bureau. Department of Natural Resources, Post Office Wards Strip, Waigaini, Port Moresby.
A wide range of maps and aerial photos. The new 1:100 000 (1km:1cm) topographic maps are particularly useful.

JOURNALS

Oceania. A journal devoted to the study of the peoples of Australia, New Guinea and the Pacific.
This journal, found in most University libraries, is published quarterly and usually contains articles on the New Guinea Highlands.

LIBRARIES

The University PNG Collection and the National Library PNG Collection.
Both are located in Port Moresby and contain copies of virtually all published material on Papua New Guinea.

HANDBOOKS/GUIDES

Papua New Guinea Handbook and Travel Guide. Pacific Publications, Sydney.
The 10th Edition 1980, contains 280 pages of detailed information about PNG.

Pacific Islands Year Book. Ed John Carter. Pacific Publications, Sydney.

Papua New Guinea — A Travel Survival Kit. Tony Wheeler. Lonely Planet Publications, South Yarra Victoria Australia 1979.
An excellent reliable up-to-date guide for the tourist.

South Pacific Handbook. Bill Dalton and David Stanley. Moon Publications, Chicago 1979.

PICTORIAL GUIDES

The Highlanders. James Sinclair. Jacaranda Press, Milton 1971.

Man As Art — New Guinea Body Decoration. Malcolm Kirk. Thames and Hudson, London 1981.

Wigmen of Papua. James Sinclair. Jacaranda Press, Milton 1973.

Gardens of War. Robert Gardner and Karl G. Heider. Random House, New York 1968.

ASSORTED

Kiap — Australia's Patrol Officers in Papua New Guinea. James Sinclair. Pacific Publications, Sydney 1981.

Up From South — A Prospector in New Guinea 1931–1937. Jack O'Neill. Oxford University Press, Melbourne 1979.

Plumes and Arrows. Colin Simpson. Angus and Robertson, Sydney 1962.

ETHNOGRAPHIC

Highland Peoples of New Guinea. Paula Brown. Cambridge University Press, Cambridge 1978.

An Introduction to the Peoples and Cultures of Melanesia. Ann Chowning. Cummings Publishing Company, Menlo Park California 1977.

Ongka — A Self Account by a New Guinea Big Man. Andrew Strathern. Duckworth, London 1979.

Cows, Pigs, Wars and Witches — The Riddles of Culture. Marvin Harris. Fontana Books, London 1977.
Contains interesting comment on aspects of Highlands culture.

The Chimbu — A Study of Change in the New Guinea Highlands. Paula Brown. Routledge and Kegan Paul, London 1973.

The High Valley. Kenneth Read. Allan and Unwin, London 1966.

Grand Valley Dani — Peaceful Warriors. Karl Heider. Holt Rinehart and Winston, New York 1979.

Pigs, Pearlshells and Women — Marriage in the New Guinea Highlands. Ed R. Glasse and M. Meggitt. Prentice Hall Inglewood Cliffs 1969.

Self Decoration in Mount Hagen. Andrew and Marilyn Strathern. Gerald Duckworth, London 1971.

Road Belong Cargo. Peter Lawrence. Melbourne University Press 1967.

Pigs for the Ancestors. R. Rappaport. Yale University Press, New Haven 1968.

Give and Take — Exchange in Wola Society. Paul Sillitoe. Australian National University Press, Canberra 1979.

Blood is Their Argument — Warfare among the Mae Enga Tribesmen New Guinea Highlands. Mervyn Meggitt. Mayfield Publishing Company, Palo Alto 1977.

The Kukukuku of the Upper Watut. Beatrice Blackwood. Oxprint, Oxford 1978.

NOVELS

The Stolen Land. Ian Downs. Jacaranda, Milton 1970.

My Mother Calls Me Yaltep. Ignatius Kilage. IPNGS, 1981.
A life story from the Simbu area.

CHILDREN'S BOOKS

Kaleku. Alex and Roslyn Poignant. Angus and Robertson, Sydney 1972.
A pictorial account showing daily life in the Simbu area.

Kolo's Family. Sue Wagstaff. A & C Black Ltd. Bedford Row London 1978.
The life of the Highlands Dani people of Irian Jaya.

FILMS

Dead Birds. Robert Gardner. 16mm

Ongka's Big Moka. David Nairn. Granada TV UK. 16mm

Pikyzaa. Nomad Films 16mm

Bugla Yunggu — The Great Chimbu Pig Festival. Gary Kildea. Office of Information PNG

Birds of Paradise. Australian Broadcasting Commission 16mm

The Mendi. Canadian Broadcasting Corporation 16mm

Tighten the Drums — Enga Self Decoration. Chris Owen. IPNGS. 16mm

Music of Simbu. Nomad Films. 16mm

Toward Baruya Manhood. Ian Dunlop and Maurice Godelier. ABC Film Australia and Nusae Del homme. 9 hours, restricted viewing in PNG. 16mm

The photographs in this book were
taken using two Nikkormat camera
bodies and three Nikkor lenses: 35mm
f.2., 50mm f.1.4; and the superb 105mm
f2.5 short telephoto. A few shots were
taken with the tiny Rollei 35S camera.

Photography in the Highlands requires
unobtrusive equipment and abundant
time. Patience is needed when waiting
for clouds to obscure the harsh sunlight.